Princesses of Heaven
The Flowers

ILLUSTRATIONS AND STORY BY
FABIOLA GARZA

Spark
WORD ON FIRE

Published by Word on Fire Spark, an imprint of
Word on Fire, Elk Grove Village, IL 60007
© 2024 by Word on Fire Catholic Ministries
Printed and bound in Italy by L.E.G.O. S.p.A.
All rights reserved

Cover design, typesetting, and interior art direction by Nicolas Fredrickson and Rozann Lee
Editing by Haley Stewart

No part of this book may be used or reproduced in any manner whatsoever without written permission, except in the case of brief quotations in critical articles or reviews. For more information, contact Word on Fire Catholic Ministries, PO Box 97330, Washington, DC 20090-7330 or email contact@wordonfire.org.

First printing, April 2024

ISBN: 978-1-68578-093-7

Library of Congress Control Number: 2023946275

To my little princess and
goddaughter, Elena Sofía.

"Consider how the wild flowers grow. They do not labor or spin. Yet I tell you, not even Solomon in all his splendor was dressed like one of these."

LUKE 12:27

Every girl is a Princess.

The King of Kings gave you a heavenly crown
to decorate with faith, hope, and charity.

Like picking flowers in a garden to make
a bouquet for someone you love, choose
wonderful deeds to adorn your crown.

*There is no princess more beautiful
than one who lives for God.*

Joan, Bakhita, Kateri, Narcisa, Lucy, and Thérèse are saints in heaven with shining crowns.

All of them are holy, yet their stories are so different from each other!

Together they pray and guide you on your journey to the Kingdom of God, helping you to choose what path to take so that one day you too can be a

Princess of Heaven.

JOAN

*Joan of Arc, Brave and True,
wears a heavenly crown of wildflowers.*

She lived in a little village in France long ago. Joan loved the King of Heaven and her country. There was nothing she enjoyed more than running free after a long day's work.

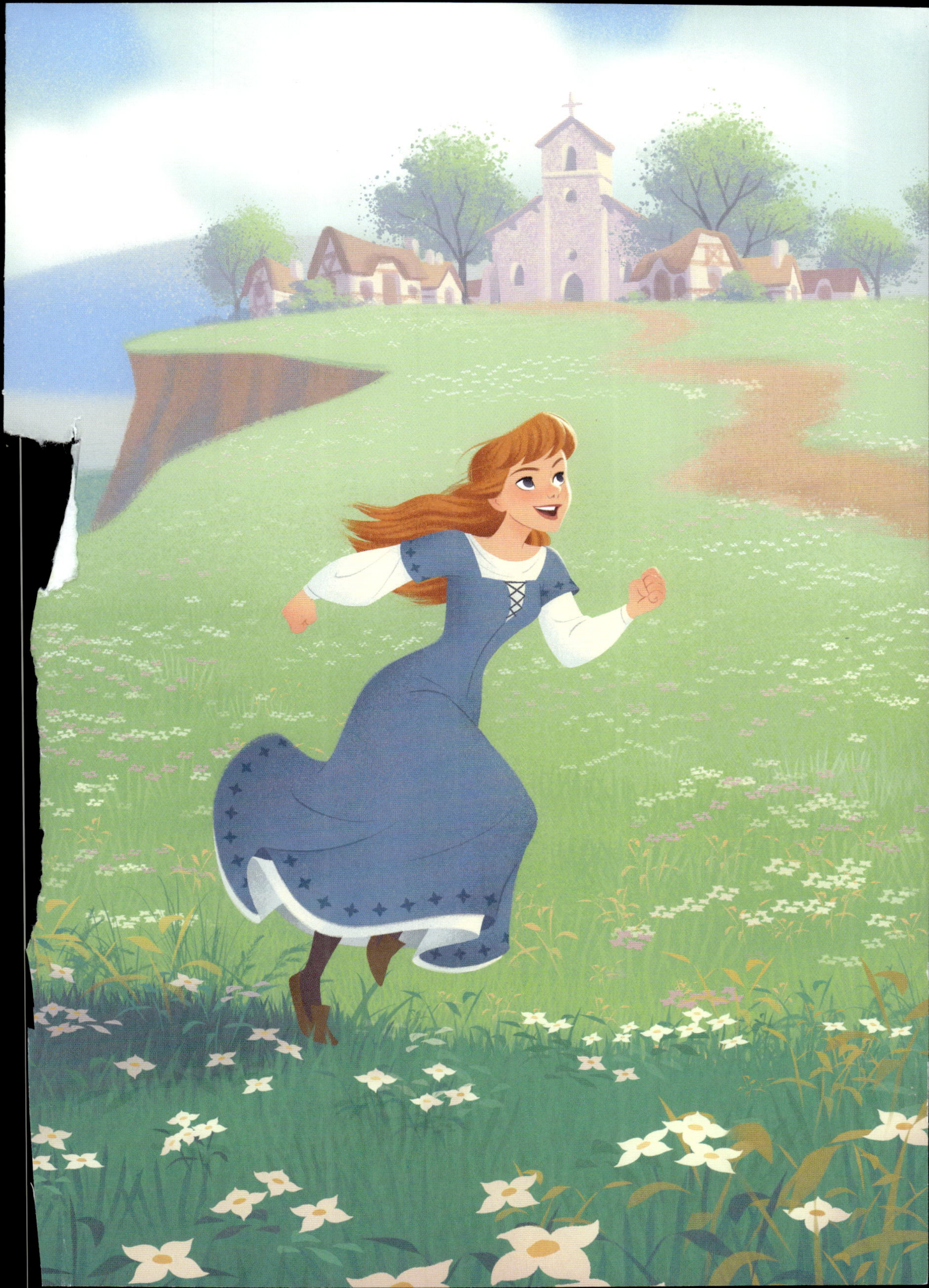

One summer day, as she prayed in her father's garden, she was surprised by a shimmering light. Three figures appeared to her: St. Catherine, St. Michael, and St. Margaret.

"Do not be afraid," said St. Michael.

"We have a special message for you. God wants you to fight for France and finally end the terrible war that has lasted a century."

"But I am only a peasant maid!" cried Joan. "What can I do? I can't even read. Why would anyone listen to me?"

"*You are a Princess of Heaven*," the saints reassured her. "God will be your guide and shield."

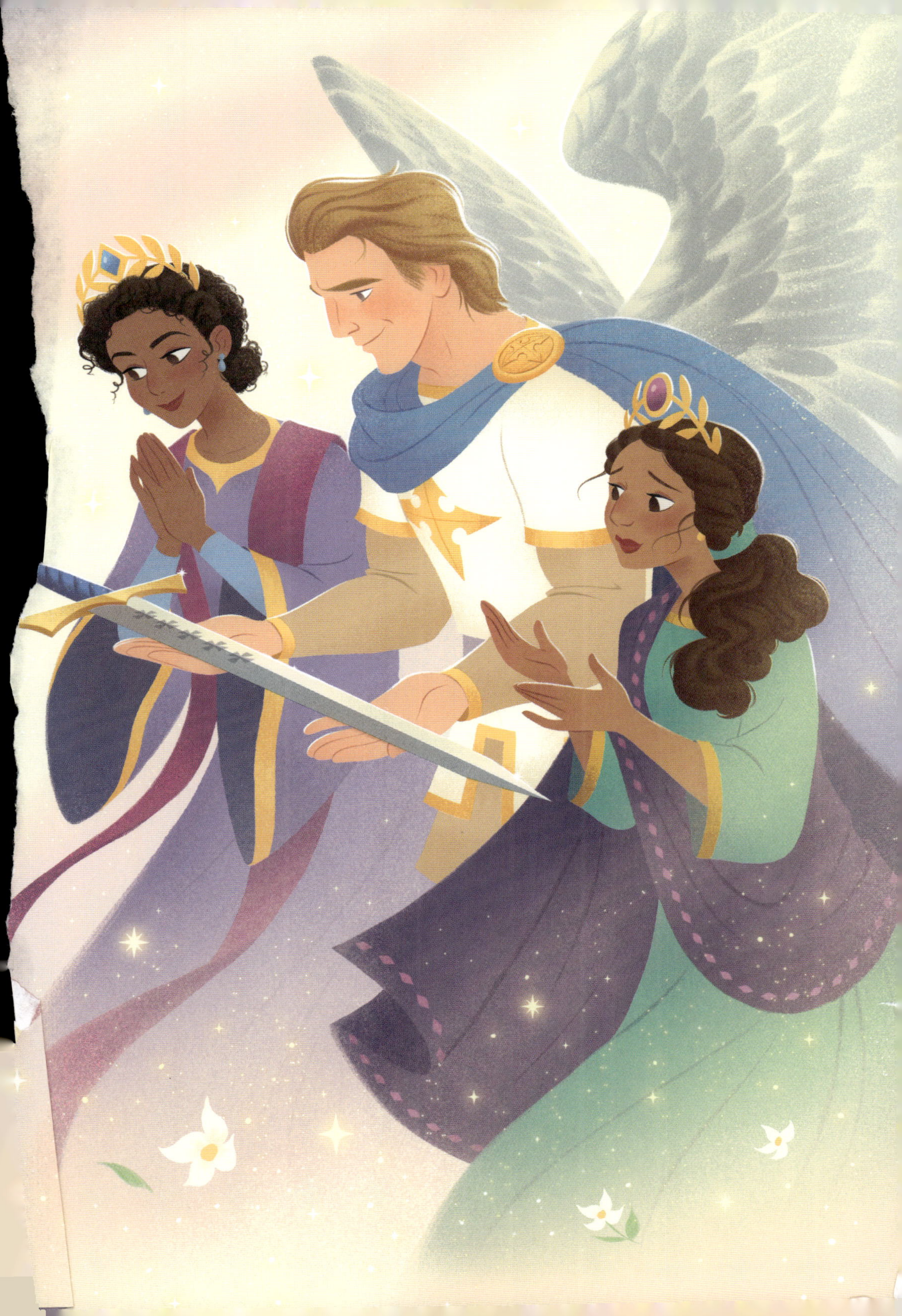

Joan traveled all the way to the royal fortress of Chinon to ask Charles, the king-to-be, for help.

"The Lord has sent me to bring peace and make you King of France," she told him. "Give me knights, armor, and a banner, and God will give you victory!"

Could a peasant girl really lead men into battle? It was too much for Charles to believe. But a sign from Heaven changed his mind, and so he said, "Go forth, young maid! I believe *you* are the answer to all our prayers."

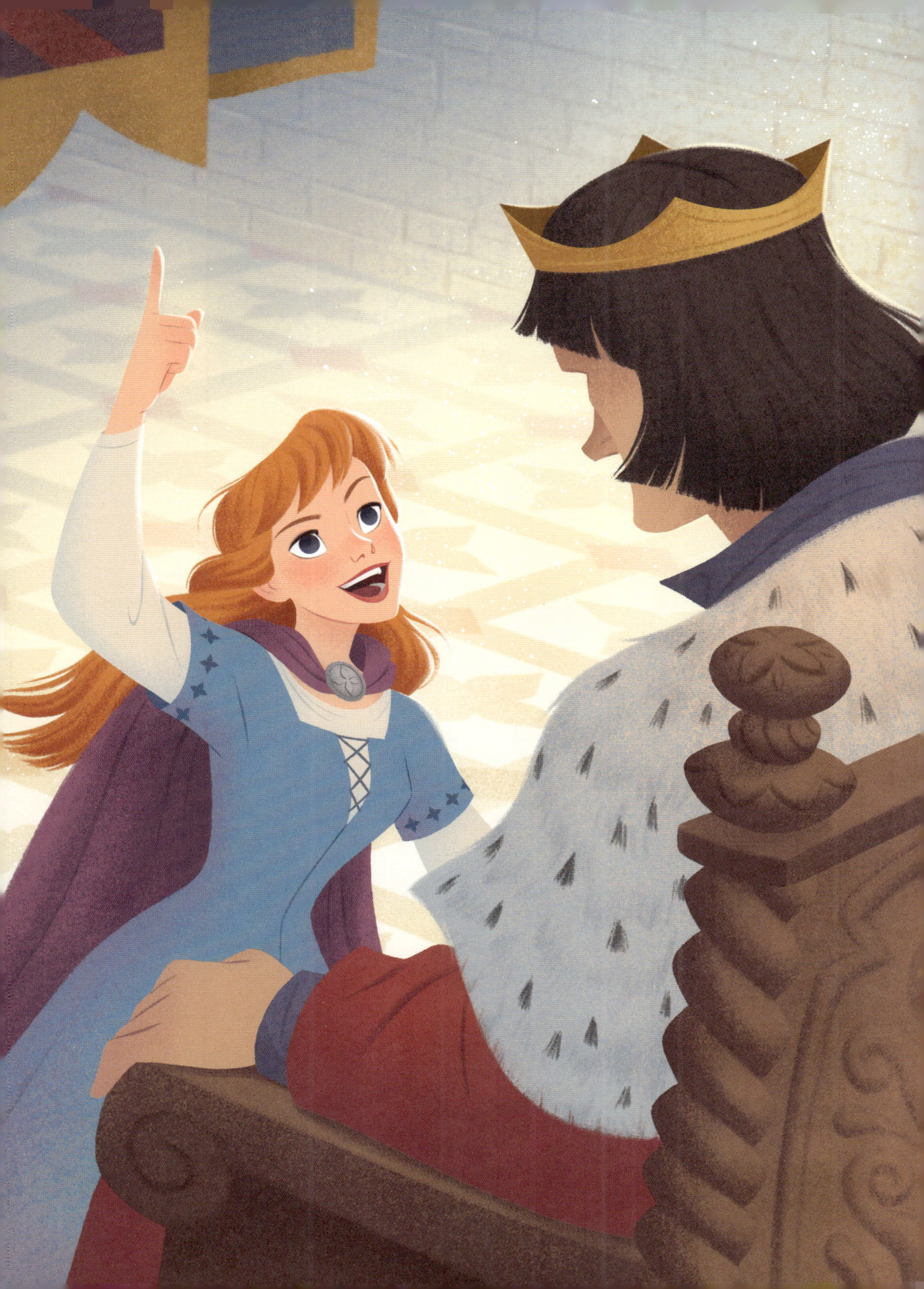

Joan led her band of knights into battle from dawn to dusk. Even when she was hit by an arrow, she rested just for a while. Then she got back on her horse and shouted,

"*For God, for France!*"

Her soldiers were about to give up, but when they saw Joan riding by, they were filled with hope and reclaimed the city of Orléans.

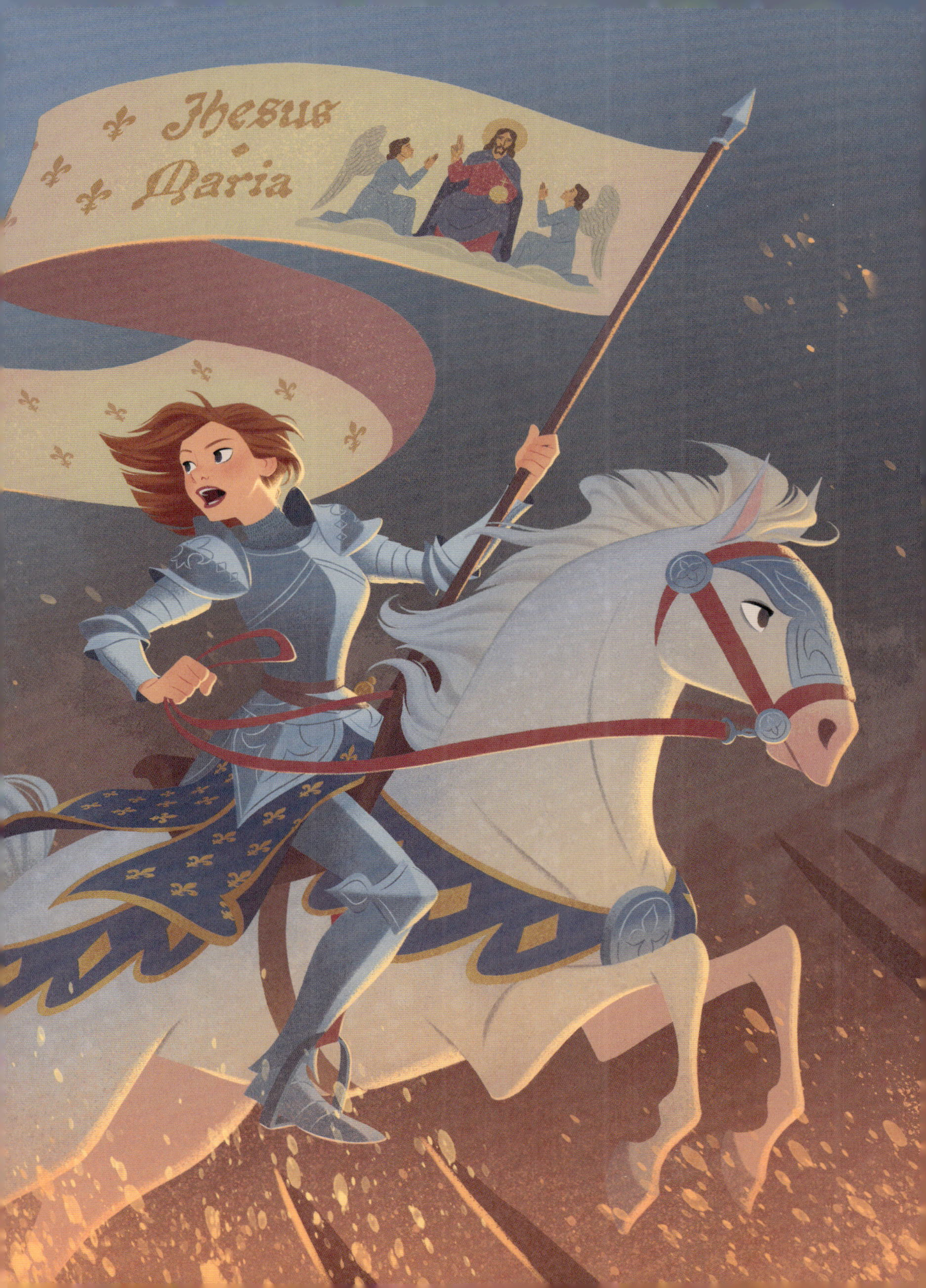
Jhesus
Maria

Joan, the peasant maid who could not read, said "Yes!" to God's call. Her courage gave France victory and peace.

*Joan of Arc, Brave and True,
wears a heavenly crown of wildflowers.*

BAKHITA

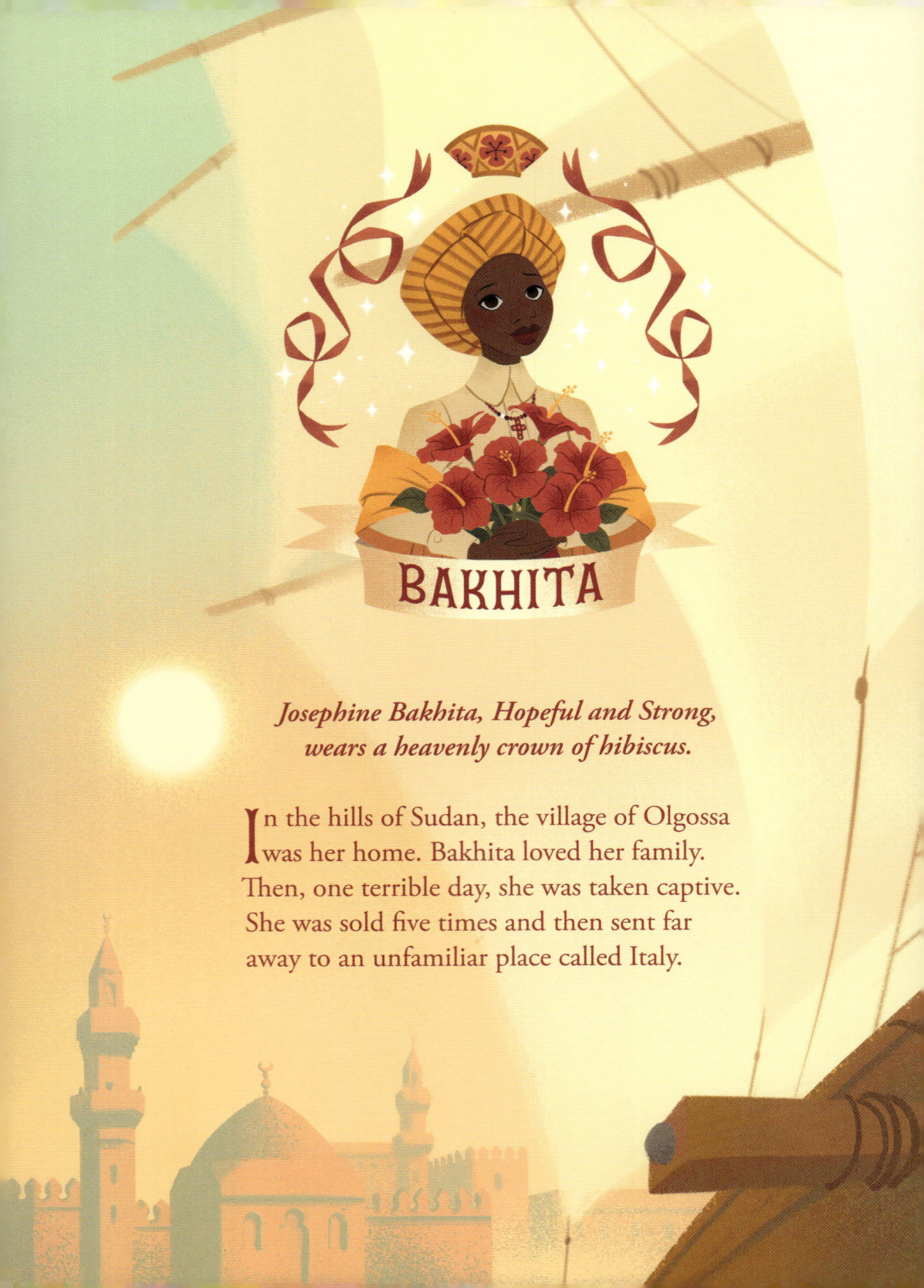

Josephine Bakhita, Hopeful and Strong, wears a heavenly crown of hibiscus.

In the hills of Sudan, the village of Olgossa was her home. Bakhita loved her family. Then, one terrible day, she was taken captive. She was sold five times and then sent far away to an unfamiliar place called Italy.

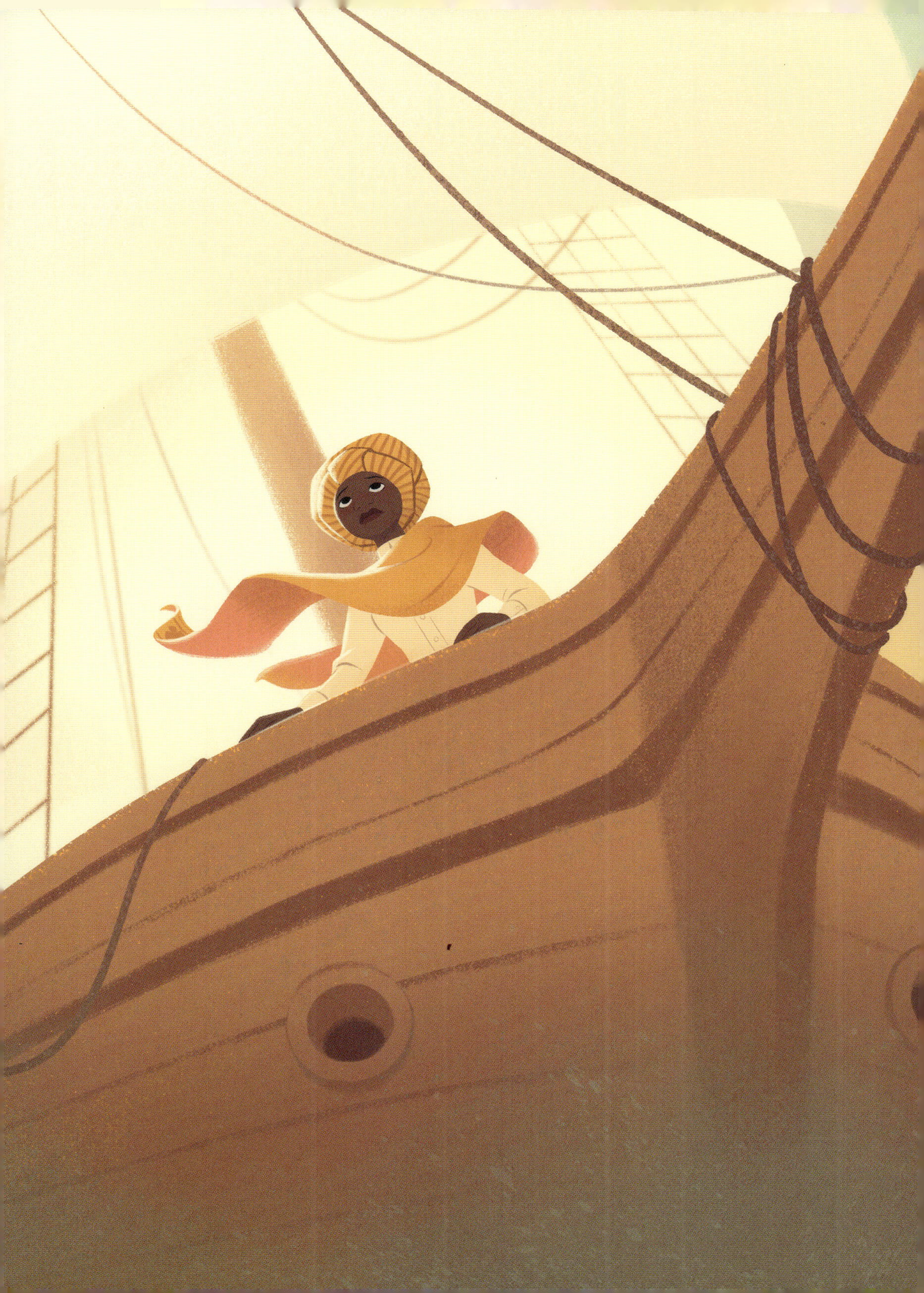

One afternoon, Bakhita asked permission to go walking through the streets of Venice with her friend Mr. Cecchini and the sisters from a nearby convent. Mr. Cecchini pointed out something that she had never seen before: a man hanging on a cross.

"Who is this man?" Bakhita asked. "He looks like he's suffered just like me!"

"*His name is Jesus, King of Kings. He died to set us free,*" her friend replied.

Bakhita could not believe a King would die to save her. But what if it was true?

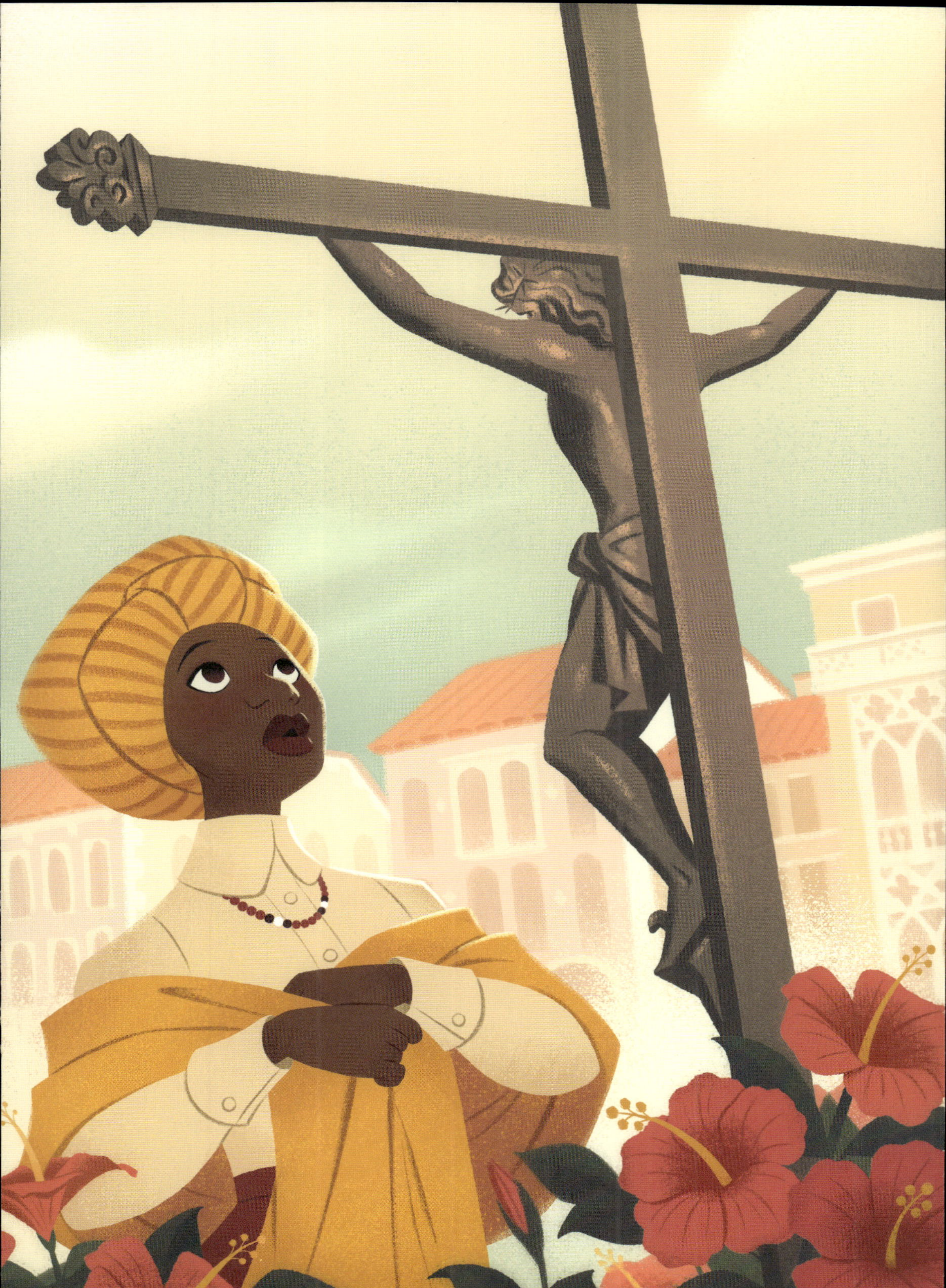

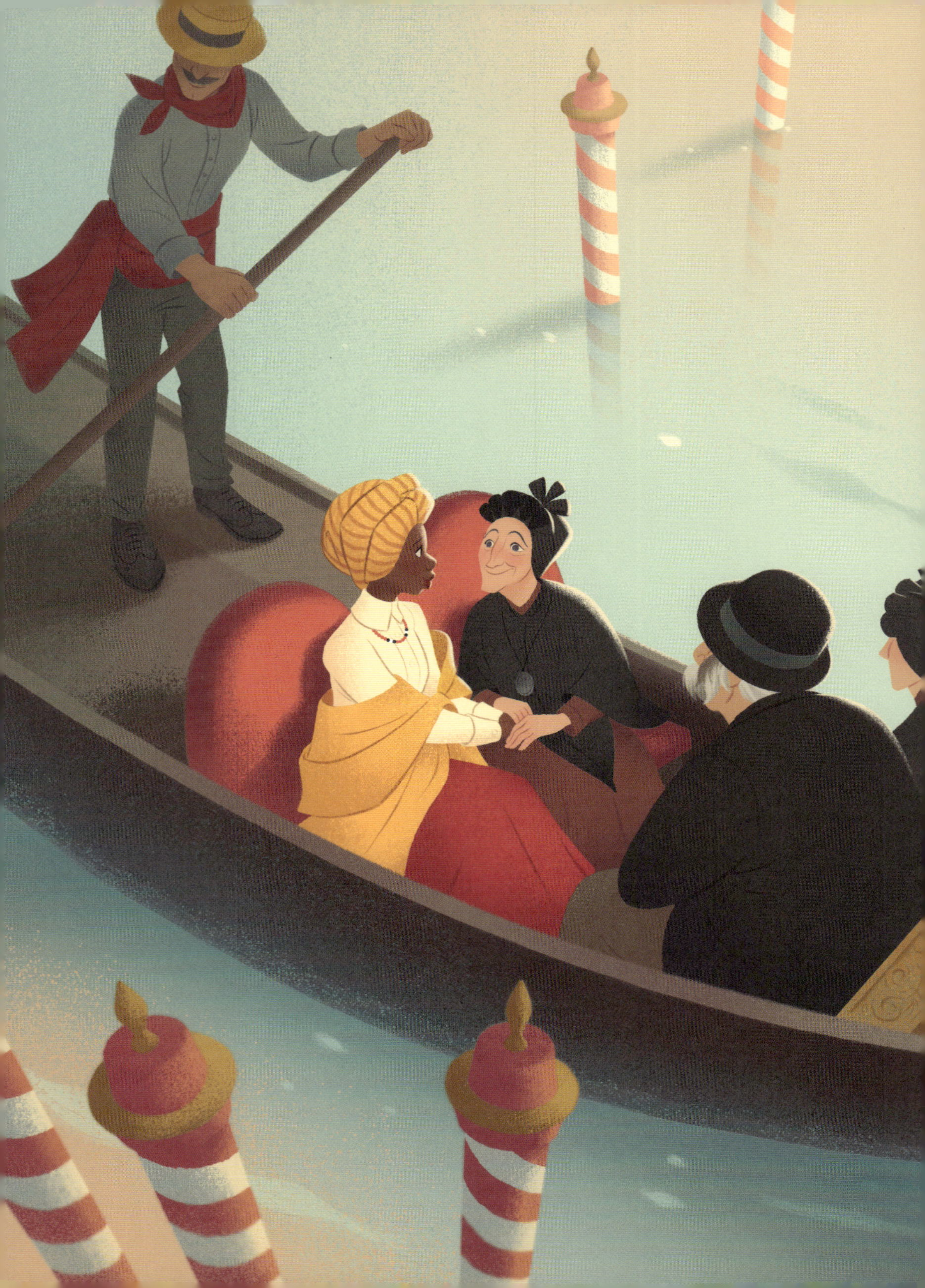

Bakhita had many questions. The nuns taught her that Jesus was even more than a King. He was God!

The Mother Superior told her: "God loves you. You are His precious daughter. *You are royalty.*"

"I wish I could be free to follow Jesus wherever He might lead!" Bakhita exclaimed.

"To win your freedom, you will have to convince the court. But we'll stand with you," Mr. Cecchini reassured her.

"And you'll have a home at our convent if that is what you choose," the kind nun promised.

The day arrived for Bakhita to defend her case so that no one could call her a slave ever again. She found her voice and proclaimed in front of the whole court, "*I am a Princess of Heaven. I have no master save the King of Kings.*"

The judge agreed. Bakhita's words reminded everyone that freedom is a gift from God that no one can take away.

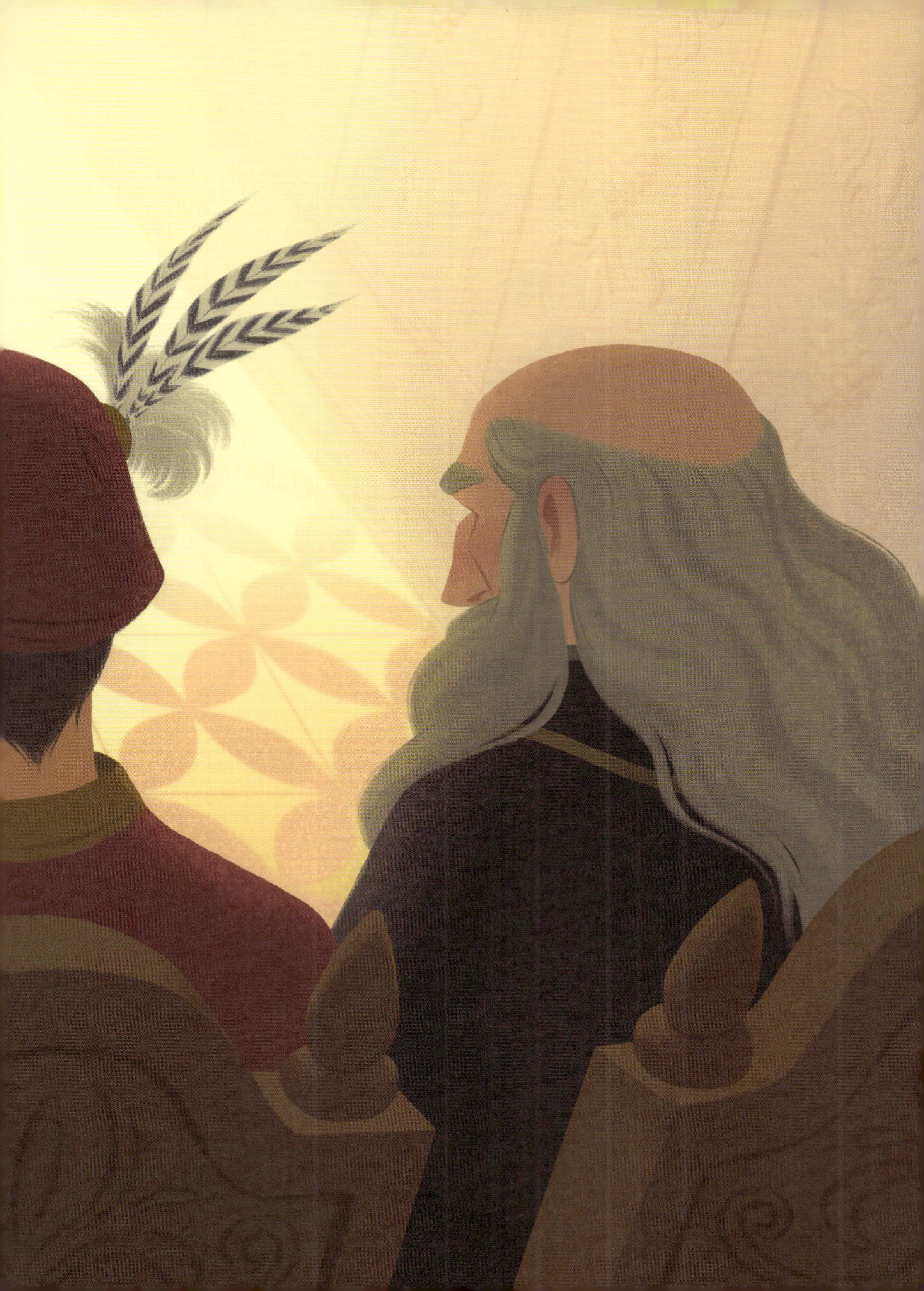

Bakhita, the girl taken far from home, met Jesus on the cross. She learned she was beloved and found her liberty.

*Josephine Bakhita, Hopeful and Strong,
wears a heavenly crown of hibiscus.*

KATERI

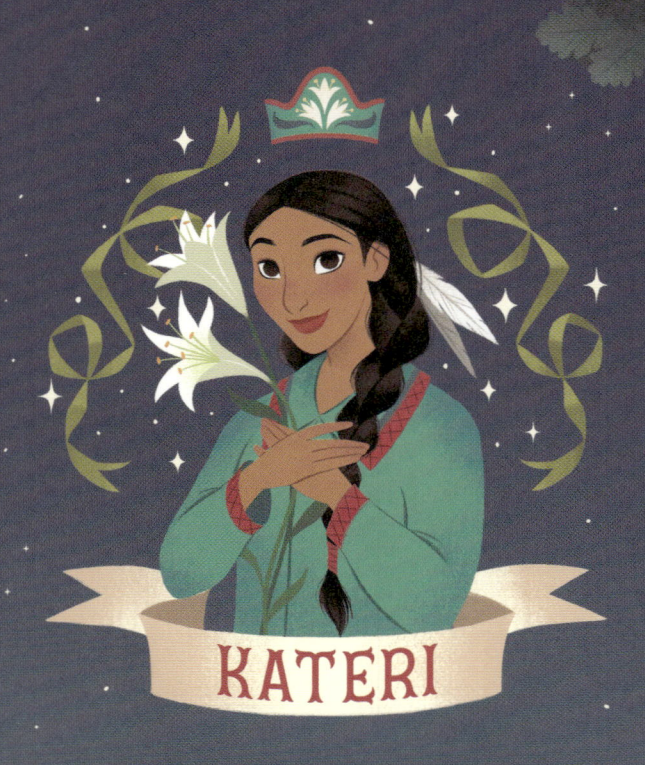

Kateri Tekakwitha, Prayerful and Patient, wears a heavenly crown of lilies.

She was born by the Mohawk River. Her parents died when she was small. Kateri's eyes were weak. It hurt to see the sun, so she preferred to say the prayers her mother taught her by starlight.

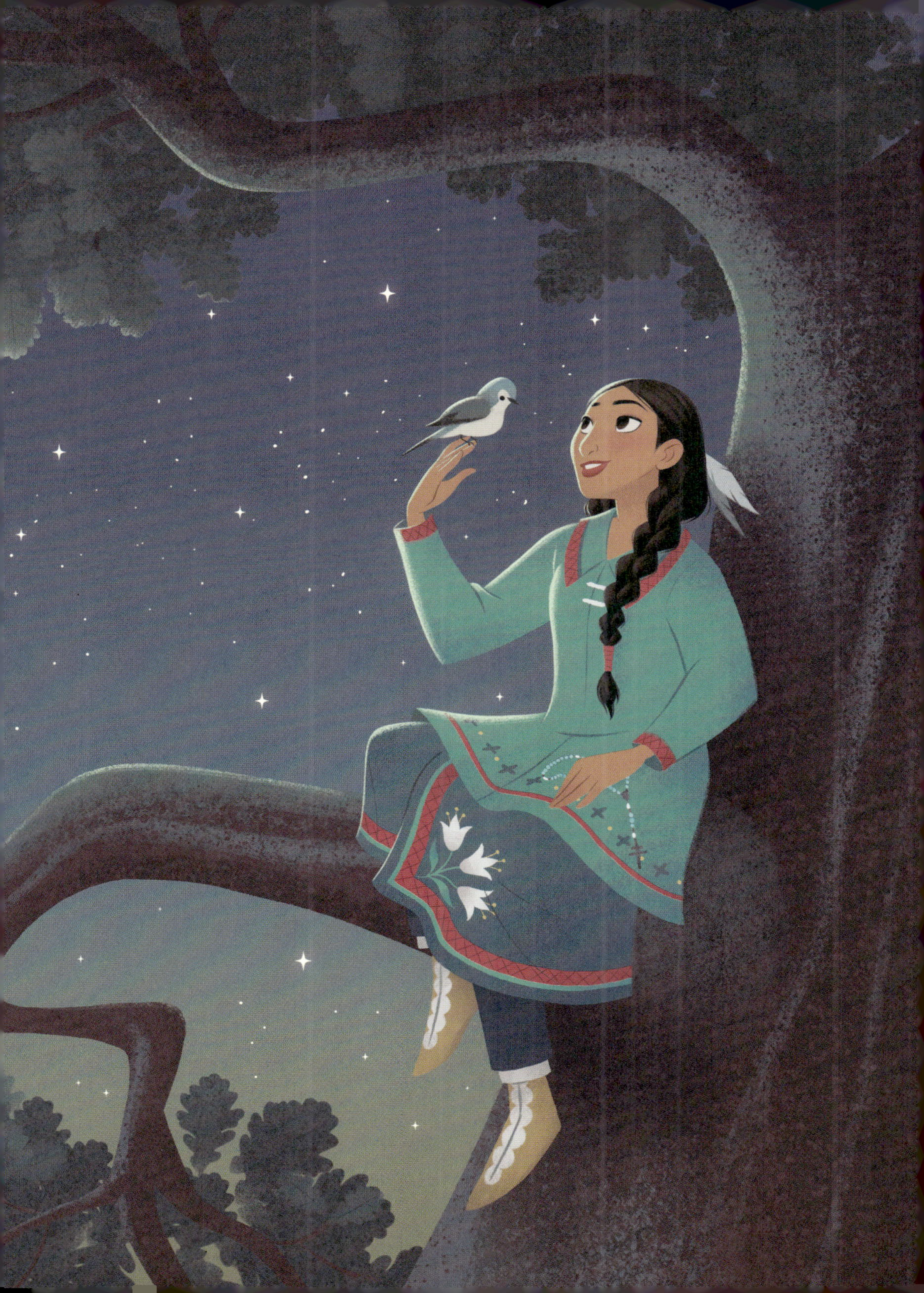

The young girl had waited and waited to be baptized. She finished all her catechism classes, and the day had finally come!

"I know it's been hard to wait so long, but your journey is just beginning!" the priest told her. "Have you decided on your Christian name, *Daughter of God*?"

"Yes, Kateri after St. Catherine of Siena!"

Kateri felt the cool water on her head and praised God, the King of Kings.

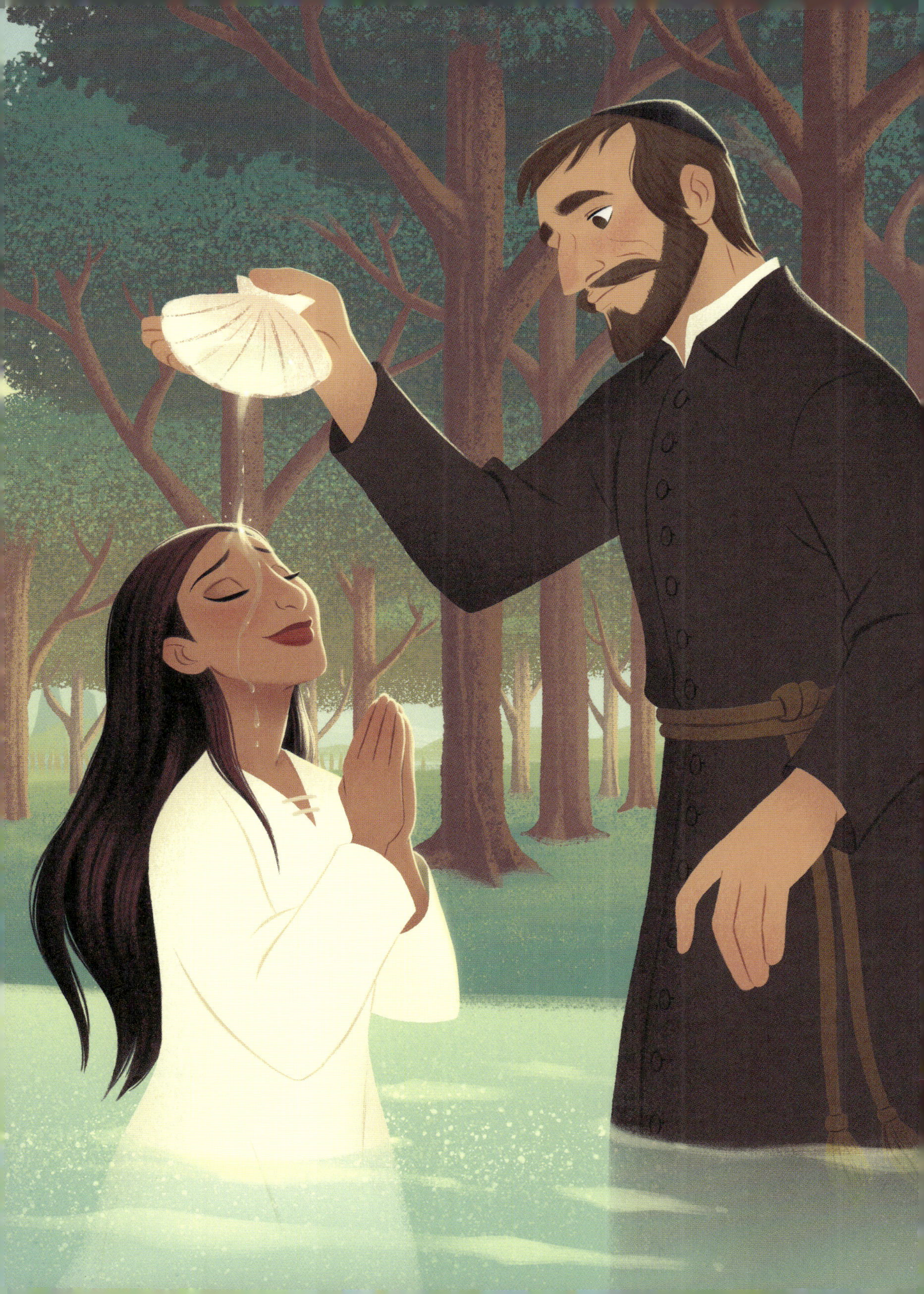

Kateri was overjoyed, but her uncle and aunts did not share her excitement.

"Don't you remember what happened to your cousin?" bellowed her uncle. "Those priests convinced our daughter to join their faith and leave our village. Now she is far, far away at the mission in Montreal. I refuse to lose you too!"

"I know you miss my cousin, Uncle," Kateri answered, "*but I must follow God's call.*"

But Kateri's uncle grew angry. She knew she must leave secretly and go to a place where she could worship the God she loved.

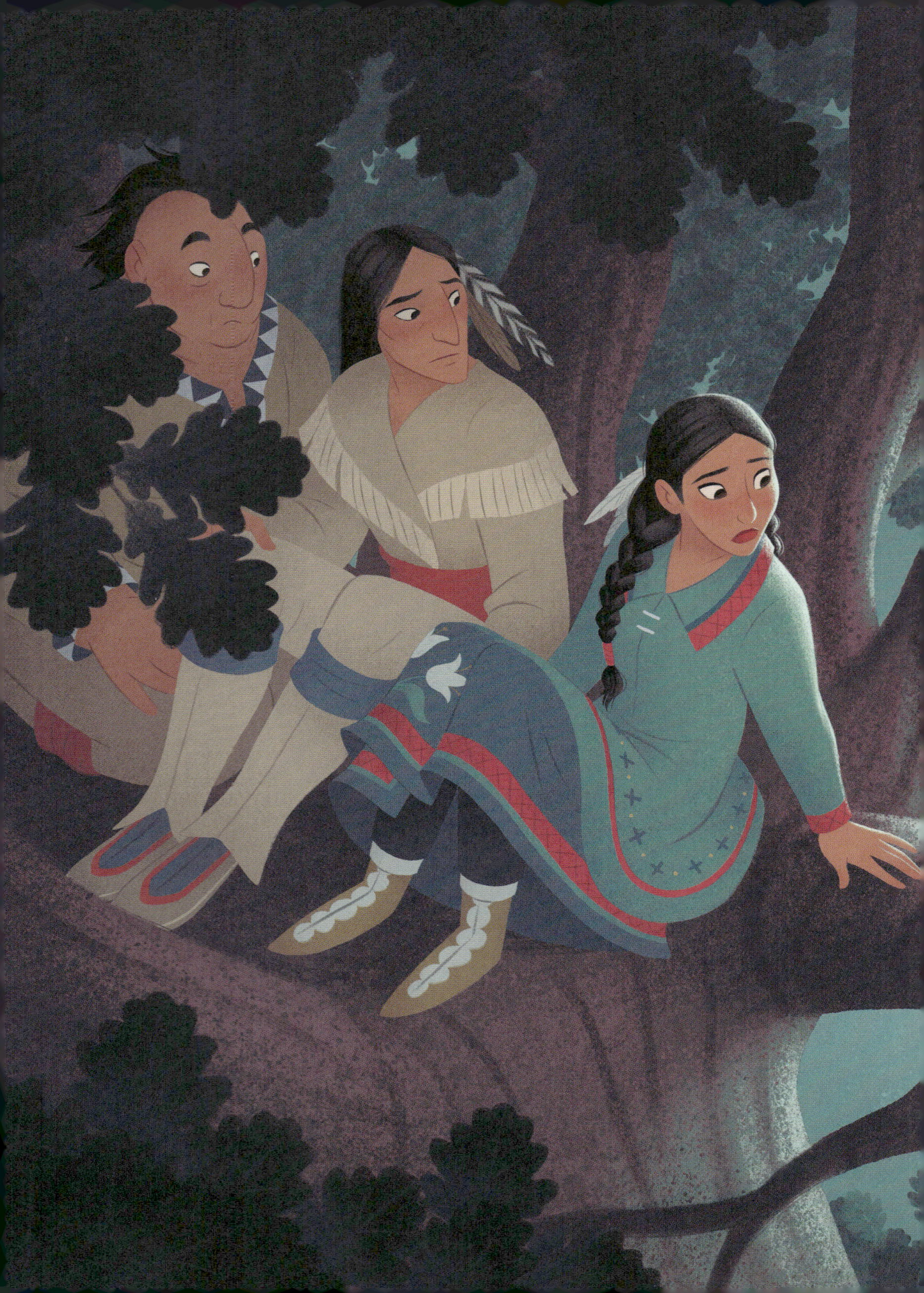

Friends from the Huron and Mohawk tribes came to help her escape. In the dead of night, they fled through the woods. Behind them they heard a twig crack; her uncle had followed them! Up the trees they went until the danger passed.

Finally, all was quiet, and they continued on their journey up north to the Mission du Sault, where followers of Jesus were waiting to welcome Kateri with open arms. As her new home appeared over the hills, she heard her companions say, *"Here you will be able to worship in peace, faithful Daughter of Heaven."*

Kateri, the orphan girl with weak eyes, had the clearest sight. God was by her side, and she followed the light of Christ.

*Kateri Tekakwitha, Prayerful and Patient,
wears a heavenly crown of lilies.*

NARCISA

*Narcisa de Jesús, Gifted and Generous,
wears a heavenly crown of violets.*

She was born in the countryside of Ecuador and lived in her family's hacienda. She loved to play guitar, and when inspiration struck, she'd sing to God under the guayabo tree.

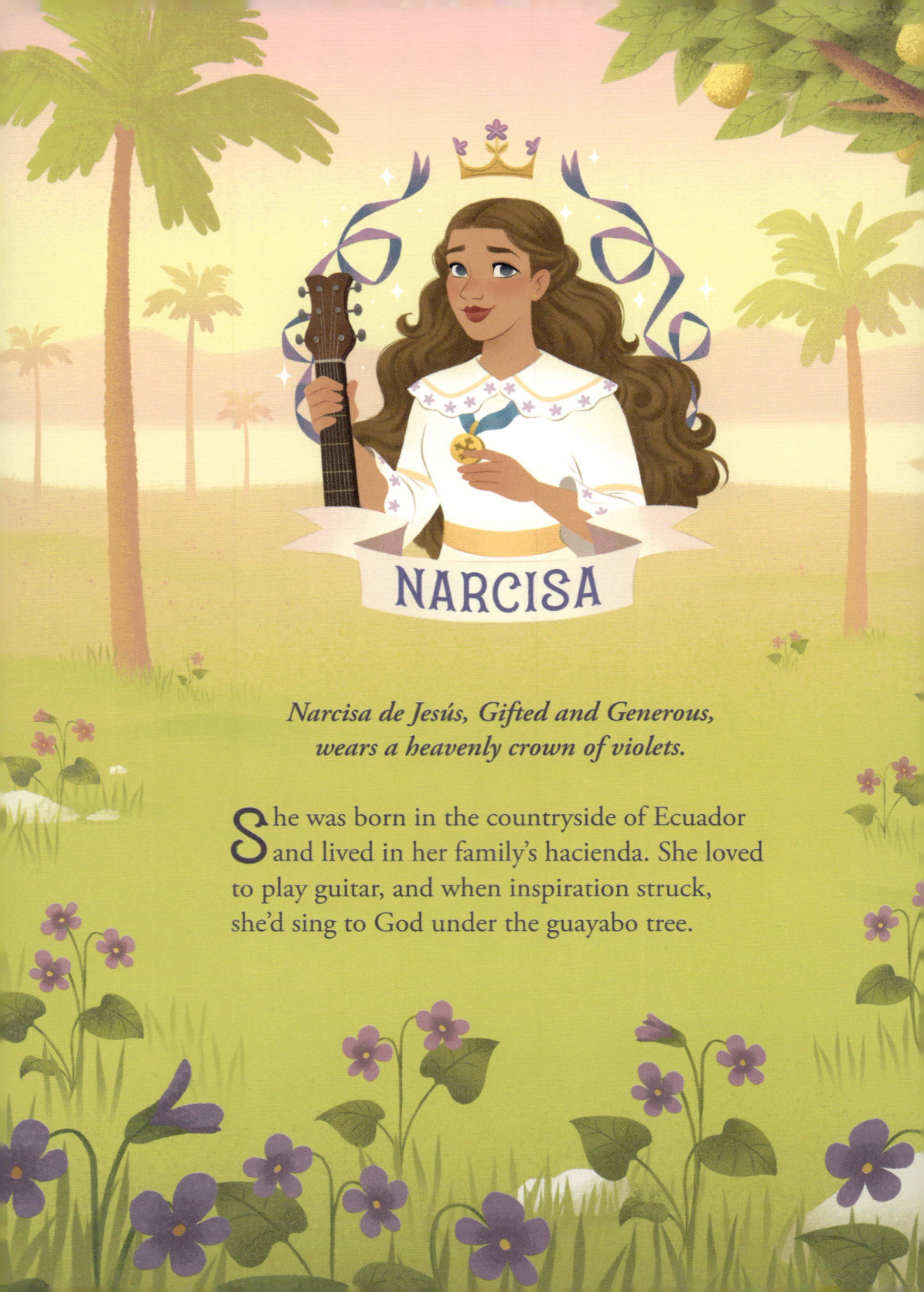

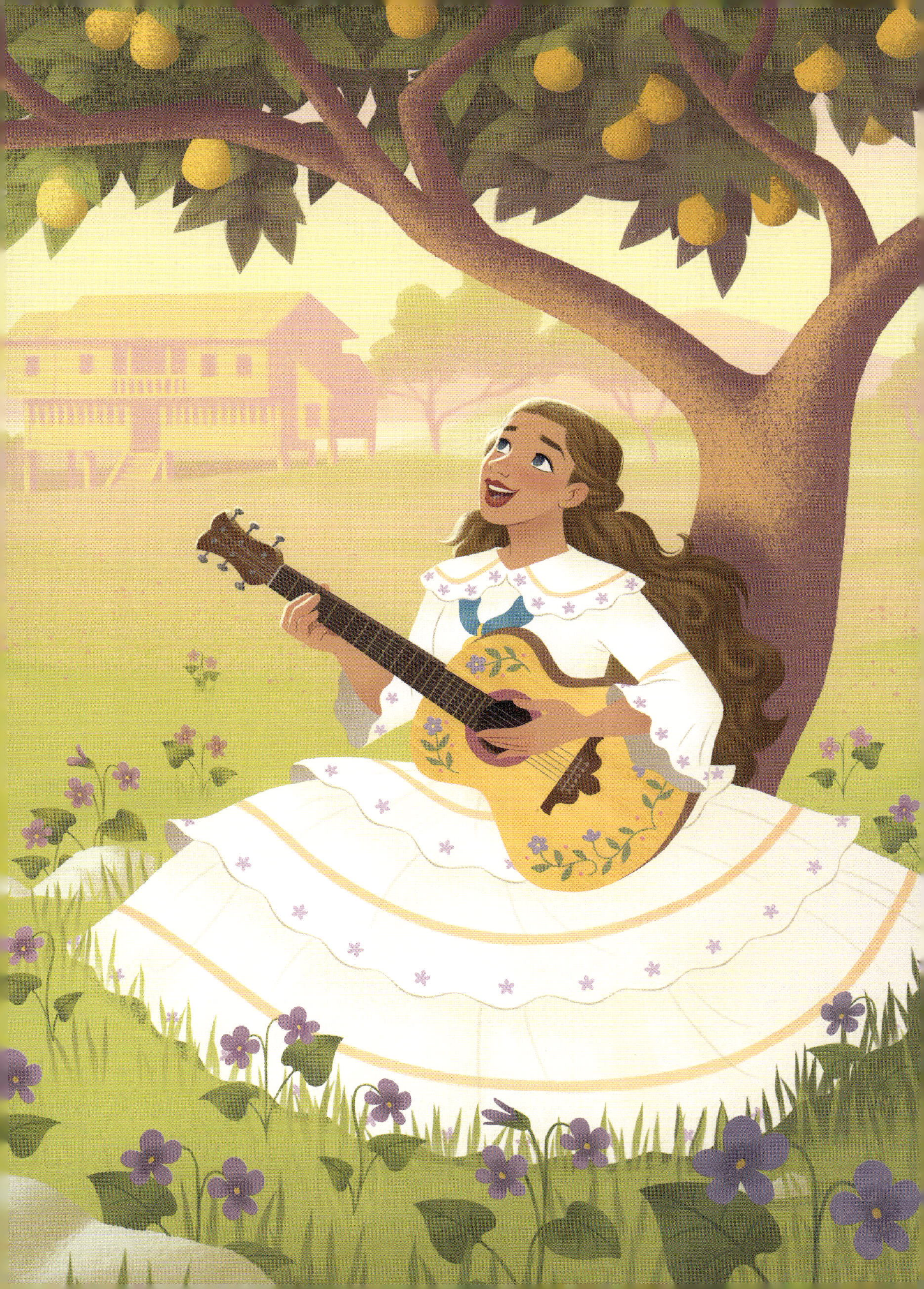

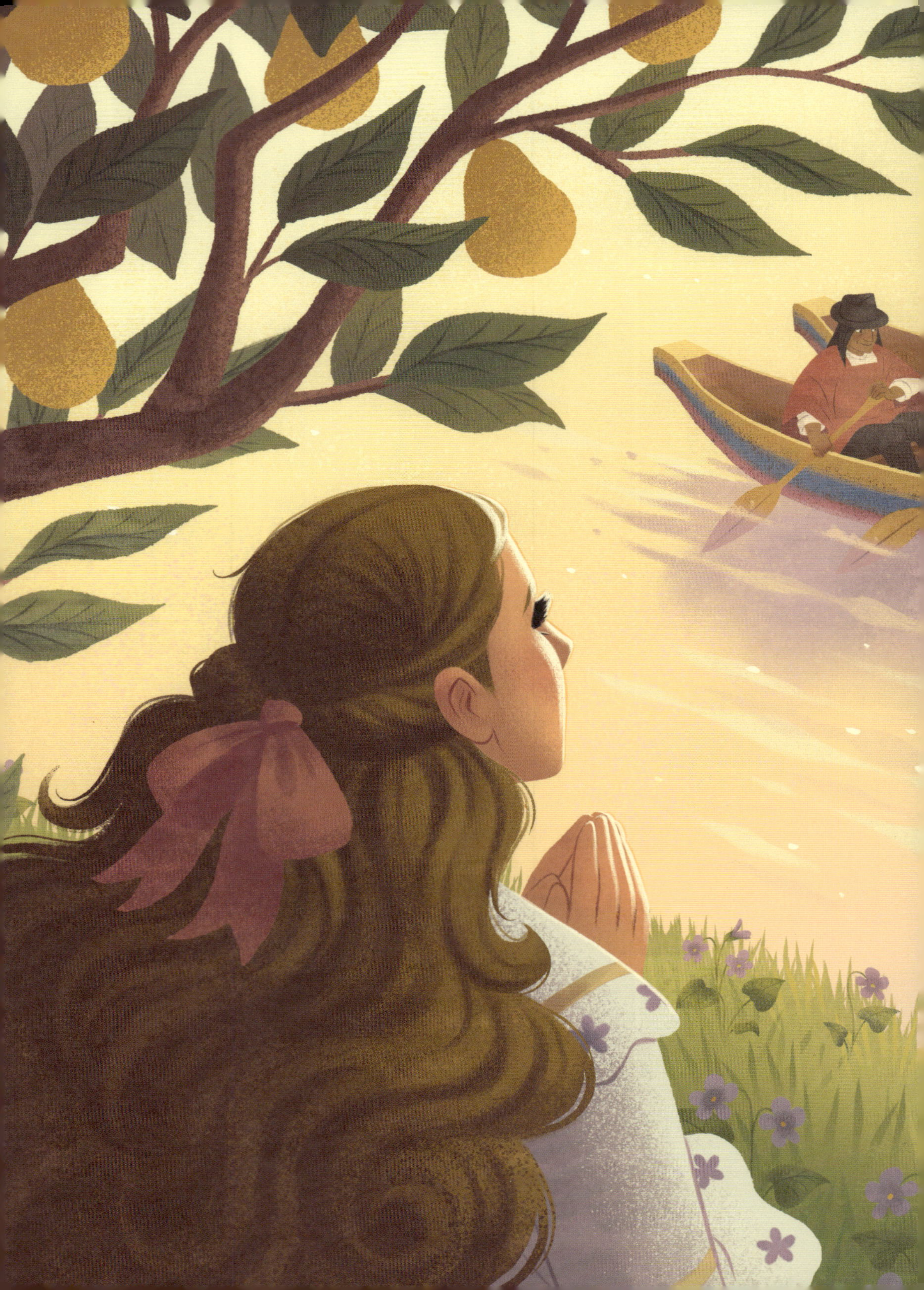

Narcisa felt the breeze on her face. All day she had waited by the river Daule to see the *Cristo Negro* come cruising down the water. In a moment, she saw the canoes. *There was Christ on the cross honored like a King.*

As the parade continued down toward the city of Guayaquil, she felt the Lord tell her, "Follow me to the city. There you will serve my poor."

"My King, I have no money. Please send me a miracle so I can do as you ask," Narcisa prayed.

Not long after, Narcisa met Silvania, a grand lady from the city. They liked each other right away and shared their hopes and dreams.

"If you come work for me, I'll give you a place to stay. Then you'll be free to pray and tend to the needy," Silvania promised.

Narcisa couldn't believe it. This was the miracle she had hoped for! But she was afraid to let God down.

Silvania reassured her, "Narcisa, don't worry! You have many gifts, but *what the people need is a princess with a heart as big as yours.*"

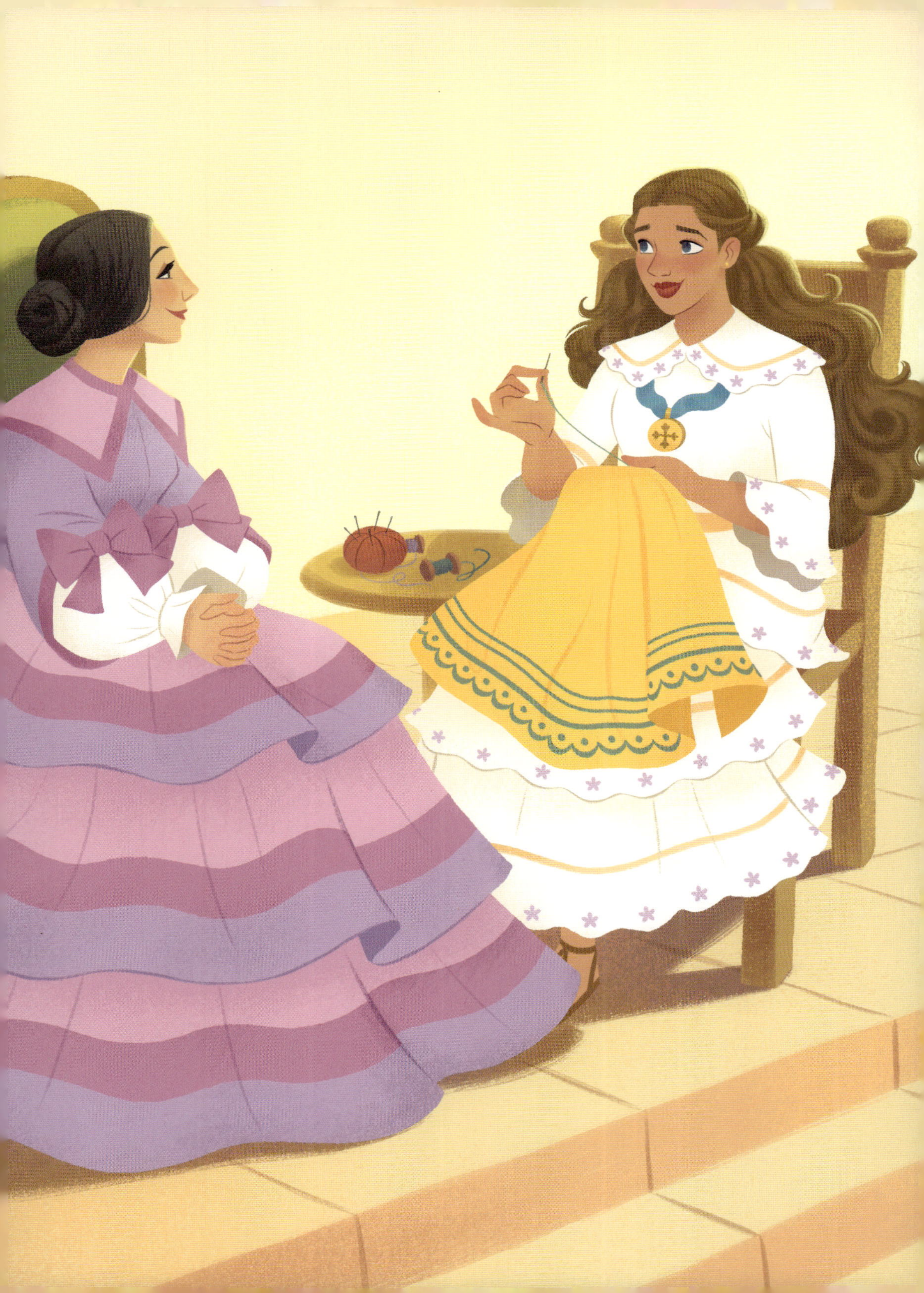

The big city of Guayaquil was crowded and loud. It was full of God's poor. Narcisa gave out bread, soup, and clothing, but still her new friends needed something more. Music always lifted her spirits, so she picked up her guitar and began to sing.

For a while, everyone forgot their worries and felt God's love. From that day, people began to say, "*A true Princess of God lives in the city.*"

Narcisa, the country girl with a heart full of song, left her beloved home to serve the poor and praise the King on high.

*Narcisa de Jesús, Gifted and Generous,
wears a heavenly crown of violets.*

LUCY

*Lucy Yi Zhenmei, Wise and Daring,
wears a heavenly crown of lotus flowers.*

She grew up in the province of Sichuan in China. Lucy loved to read for hours about the world God made. She never stopped to look at the time until her mother called her inside.

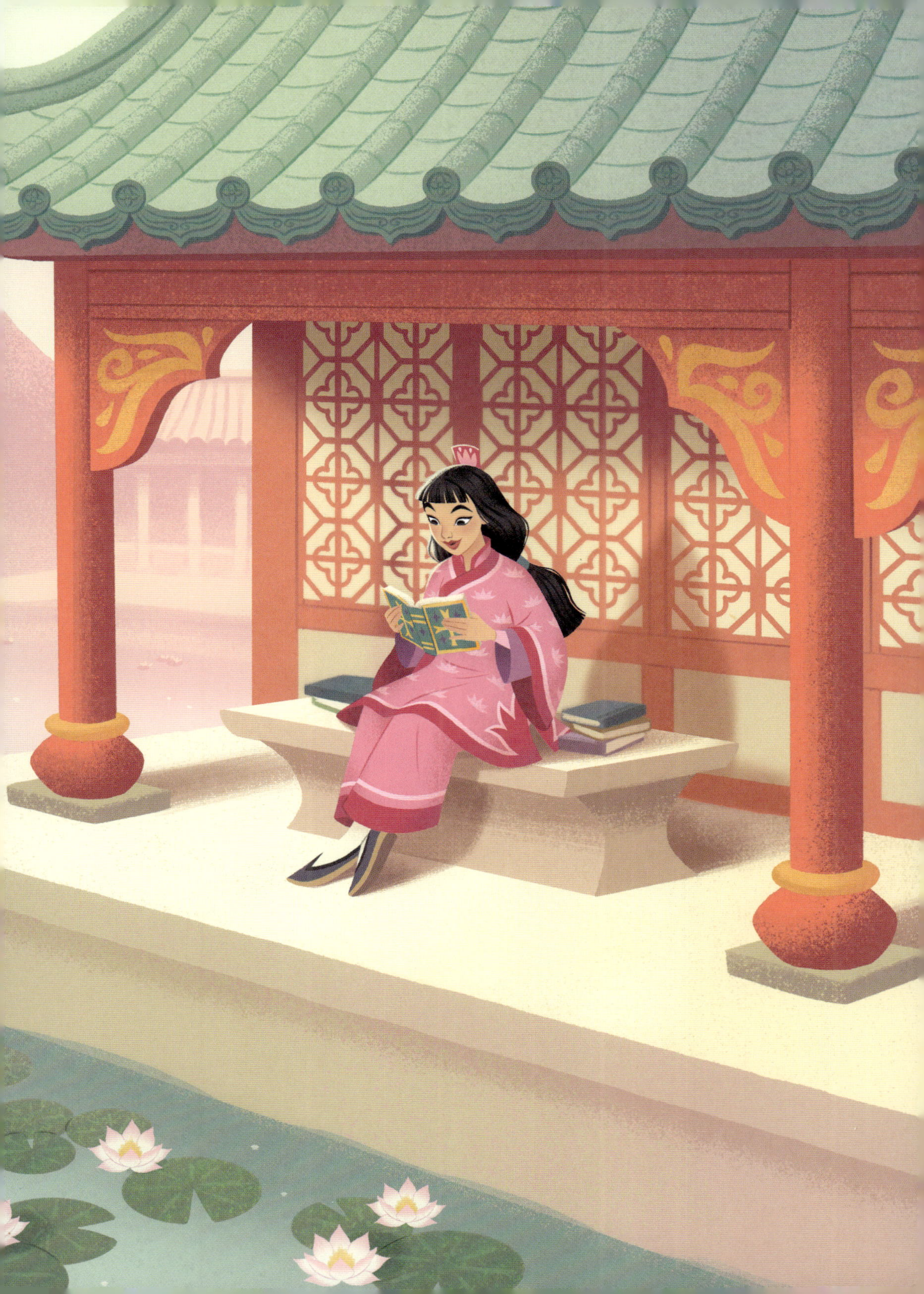

One day Lucy got caught in a monsoon! She walked home soaking wet, and for days and days, she was sick in bed. She spent that time memorizing her Bible.

"I've spent so much time learning about the King of Heaven. But I've never taught anyone about Him," she told her brother.

"It's too dangerous, Lucy! The new magistrate has been putting Christians in jail. Can't you teach something else? *You are the smartest girl I know*. Too smart to risk your life!" he warned.

Lucy loved her brother, but she knew it was time to stop hiding behind her books.

The local priest was walking to the market when he saw Lucy talking to the neighborhood children.

"Riches will not make you happy," she was telling them. "Only God's love can make you happy. *In his eyes we are all princes and princesses.*"

"Lucy! It's not safe to preach in the open," the good priest warned. "Why don't you come to the school and teach there instead?"

Her eyes lit up, and she responded eagerly, "That would be a dream come true!"

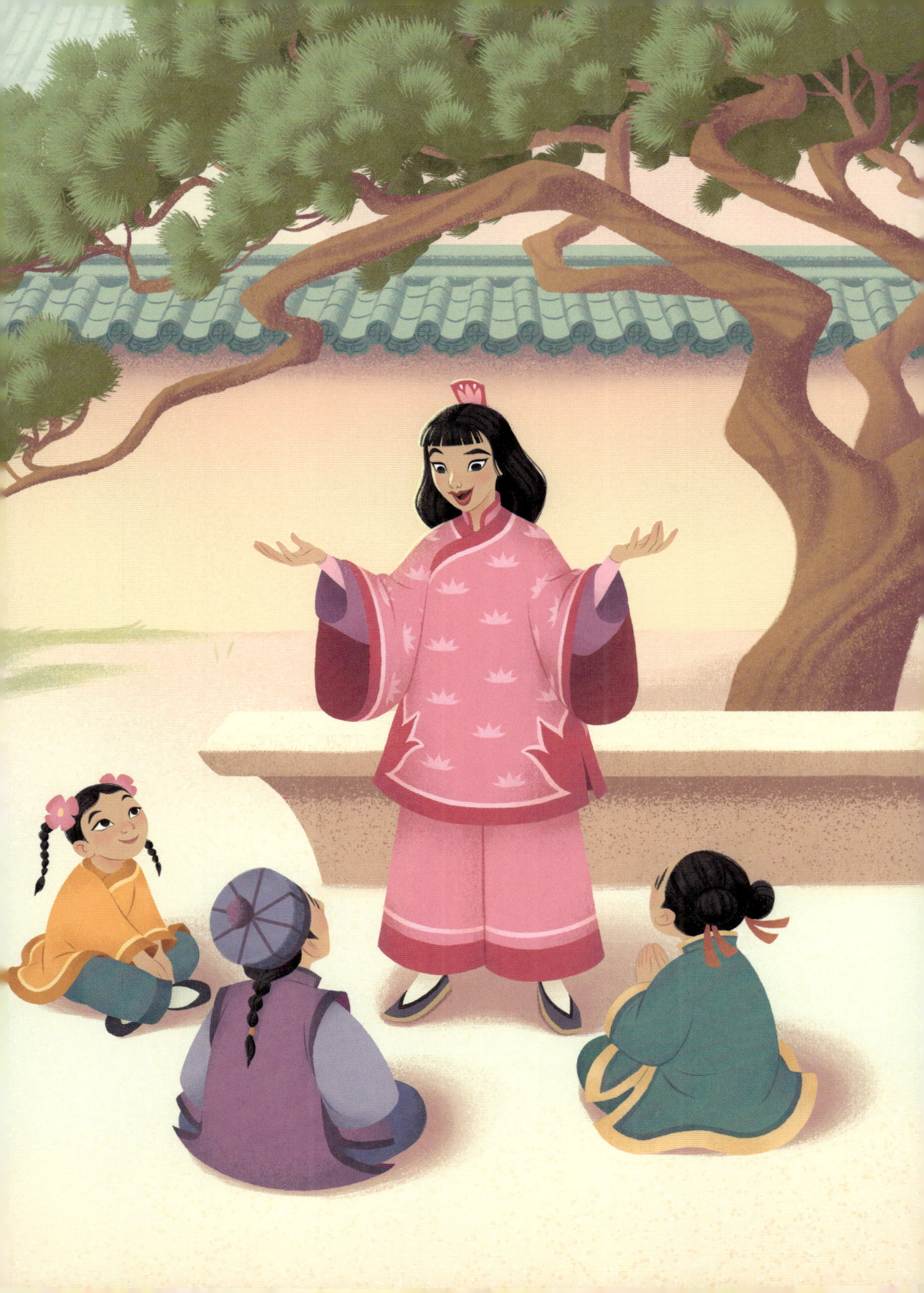

On the way to her first lesson, Lucy tripped in the busy street. A boy saw her forbidden Bible, grabbed it, and said, "I bet I can get a reward for turning you in."

Lucy stood up confidently. "Give the book back," she demanded. "And in return, *I'll give you knowledge worth more than all the emperor's gold.*"

What could be worth more than the royal treasure? Lucy had awakened his curiosity. When Lucy offered her hand, he offered his back.

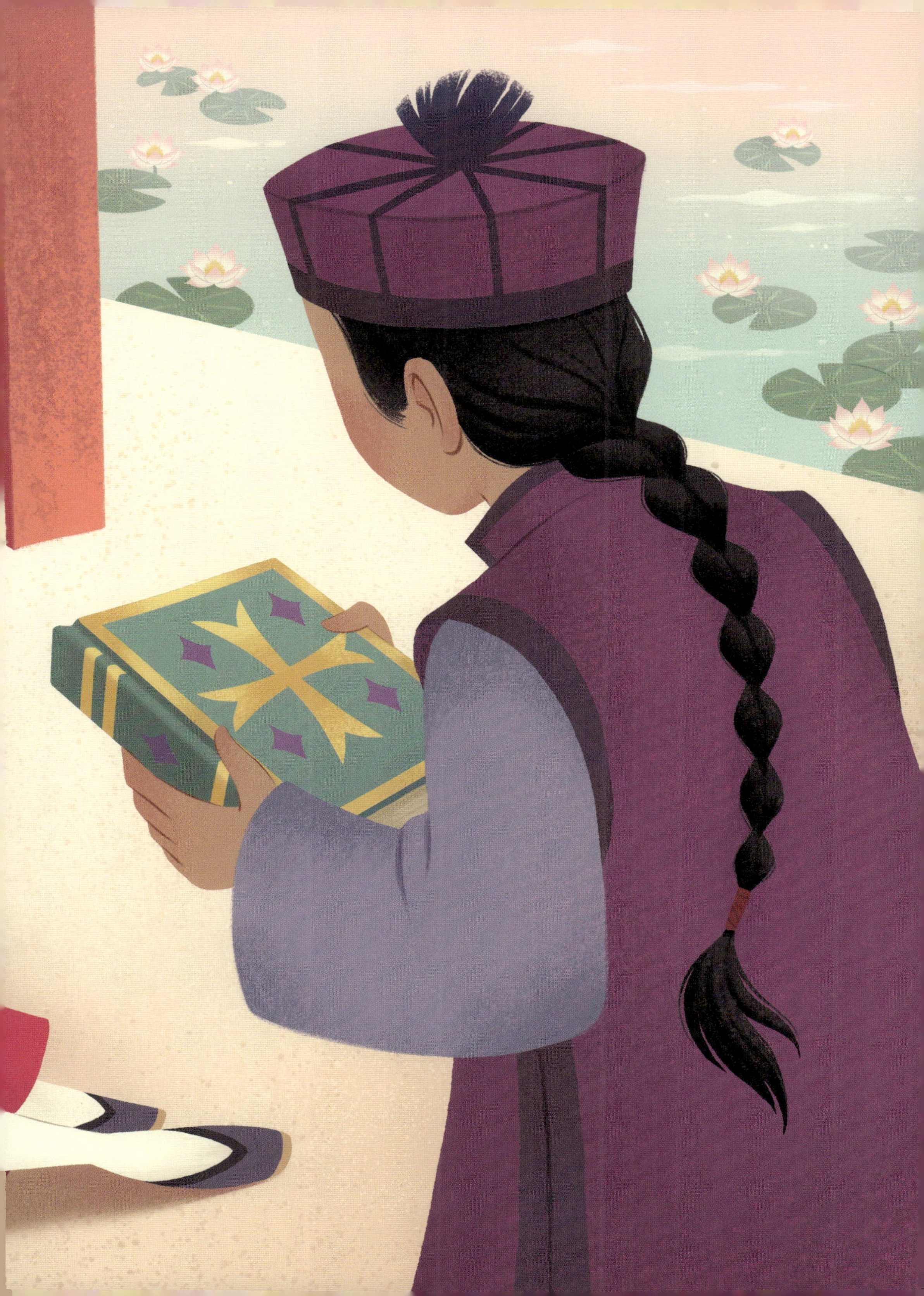

Lucy, the girl whose nose was always in a book, stepped out in faith. And despite the danger, she told the King of Heaven's story.

*Lucy Yi Zhenmei, Wise and Daring,
wears a heavenly crown of lotus flowers.*

THÉRÈSE

*Thérèse of Lisieux, Loving and Spirited,
wears a heavenly crown of roses.*

She lived in France in a little house on a hilltop. The garden was her palace. After her mother's death, her family was her safe embrace. But one by one her sisters left to enter the convent.

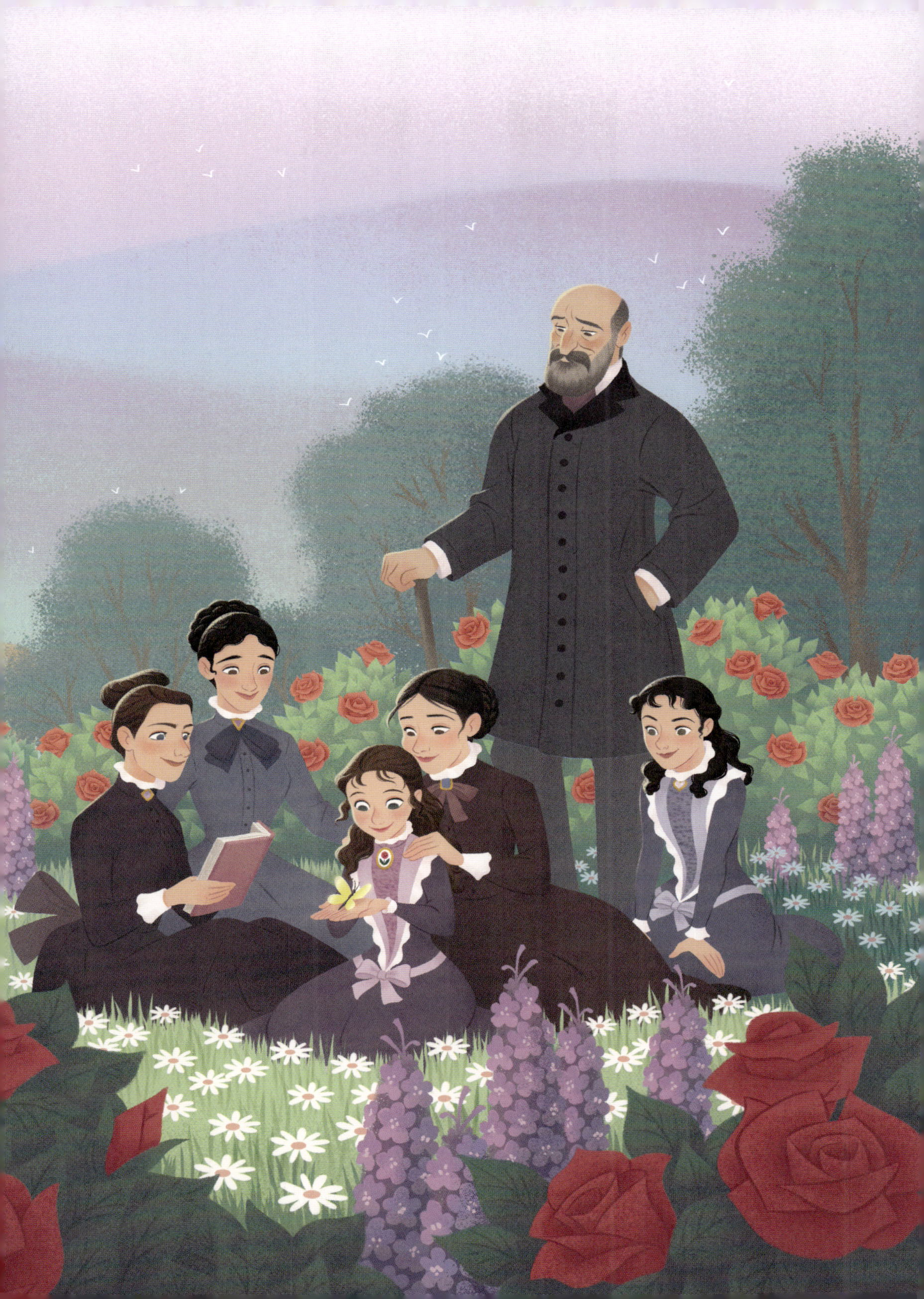

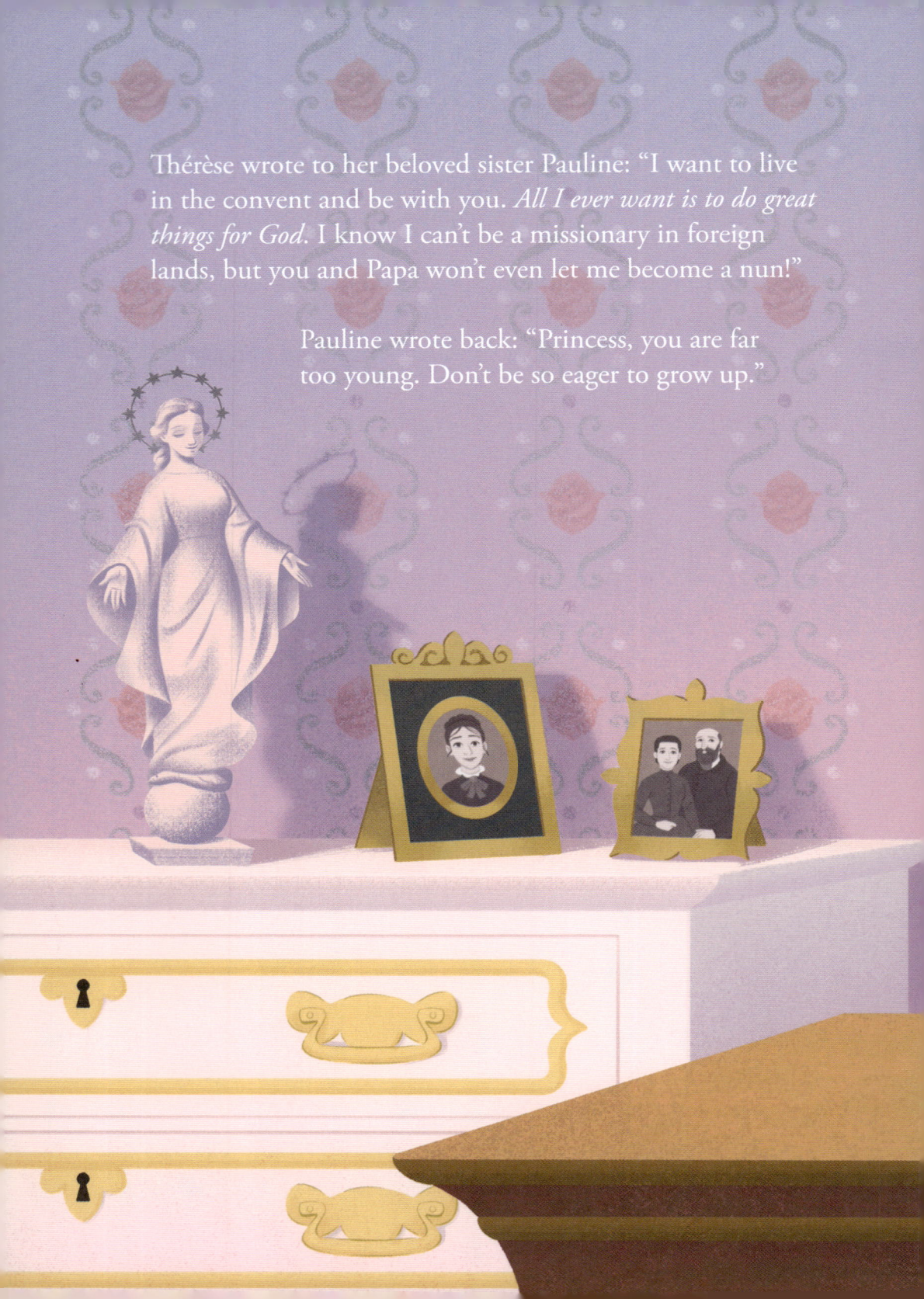

Thérèse wrote to her beloved sister Pauline: "I want to live in the convent and be with you. *All I ever want is to do great things for God.* I know I can't be a missionary in foreign lands, but you and Papa won't even let me become a nun!"

Pauline wrote back: "Princess, you are far too young. Don't be so eager to grow up."

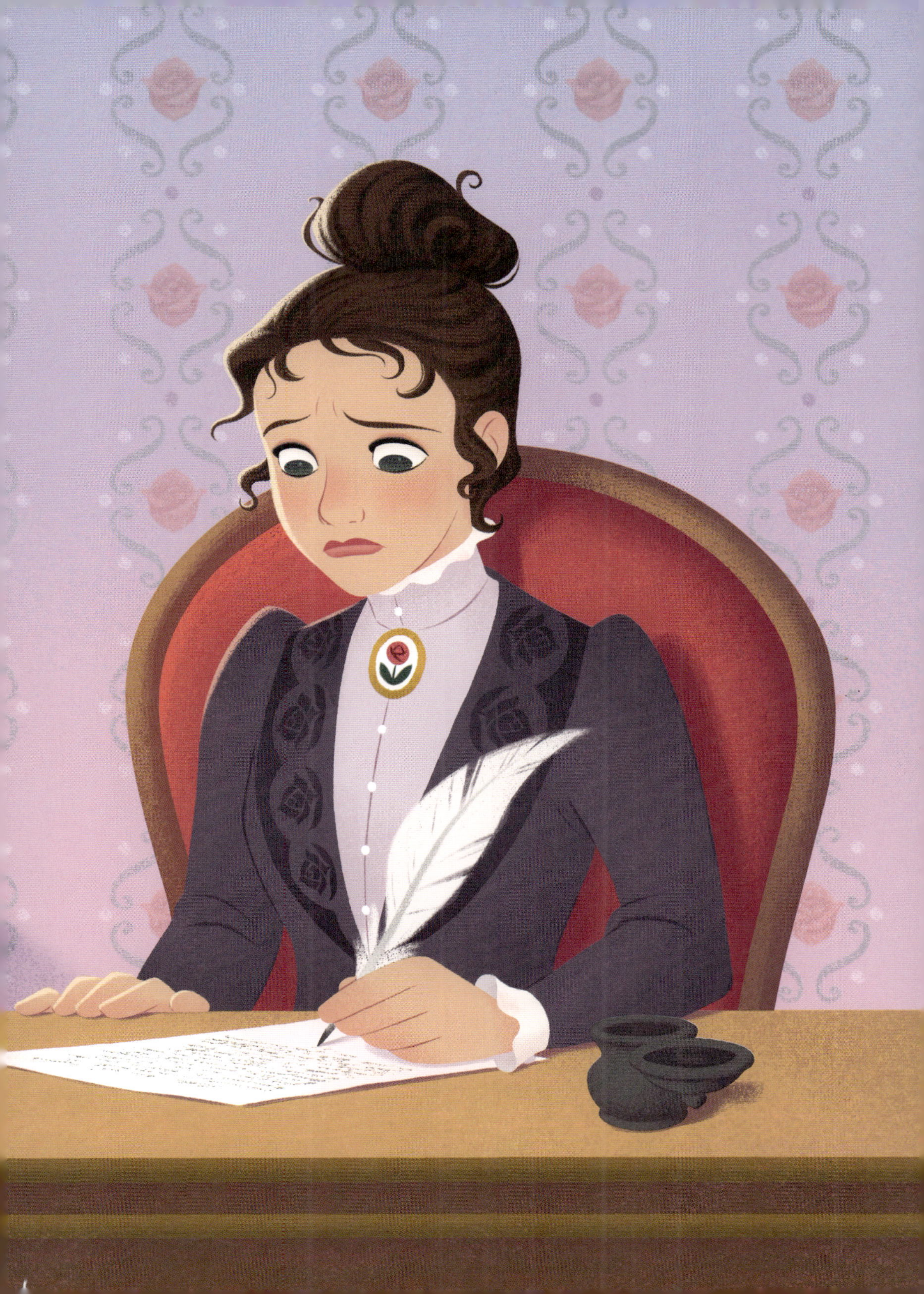

Thérèse did not give up. She went on a pilgrimage to Rome and begged the pope himself to let her become a Carmelite nun, a bride of Christ.

He responded with kindness, "Little Flower, do not be so eager to bloom. Trust the ones who love you. You can be a saint wherever you are. *Your home can be the castle where you serve Christ the King.*"

Devastated, she wept and could not move. A guard had to help her leave the room.

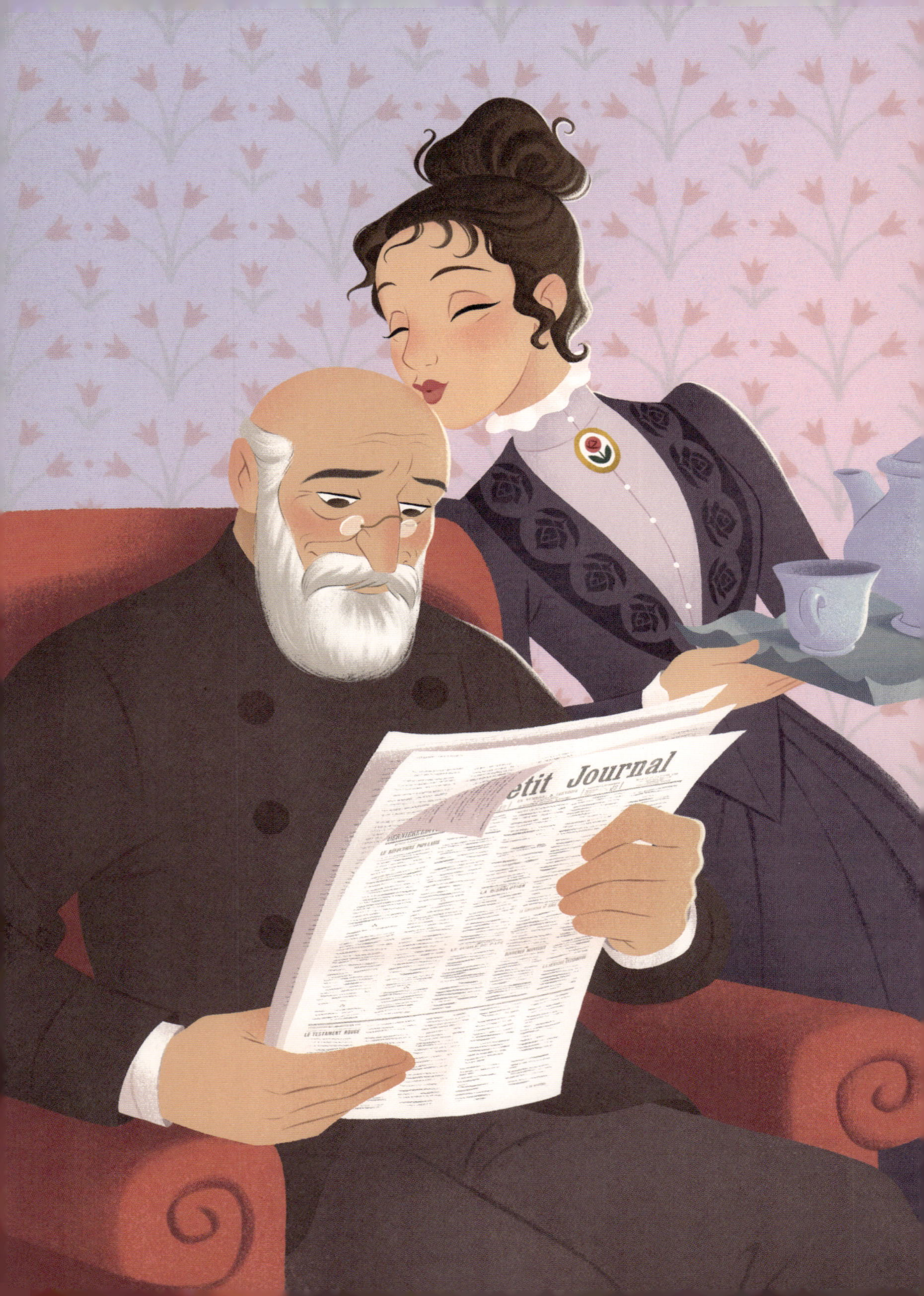
etit Journal

Thérèse went home and, despite her disappointment, took the pope's advice to heart. She found little ways to love God. When she made her bed, she'd say, "For the poor."

When she kissed her father, she'd lift up a prayer for all the orphans. And when she tended the garden, she'd pray, "For all those who are alone."

Thérèse was finally at peace. Then one day a letter arrived from the convent that made her jump for joy. It read:

> *Congratulations, Princess of Heaven!*
> *The convent is waiting for you.*

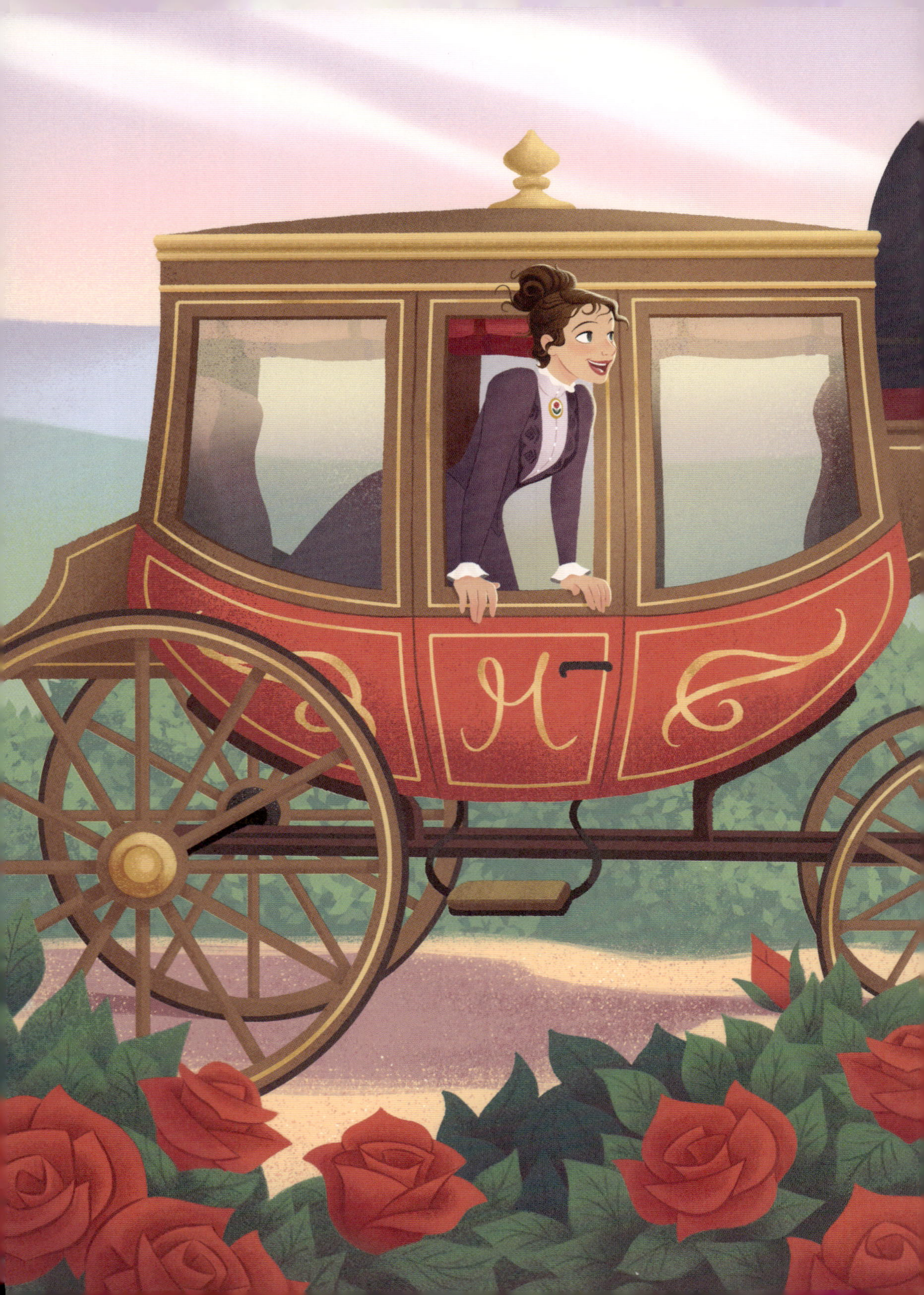

Thérèse, the girl who felt left behind, trusted God to make her bloom in His own time.

*Thérèse of Lisieux, Loving and Spirited,
wears a heavenly crown of roses.*

Joan heeded God's call.

Bakhita embraced Christ's love.

Kateri prayed night and day.

PRINCESS, what i

Narcisa gave hope with song.

Lucy shared God's word.

Thérèse loved in little ways.

our path to Heaven?

Pronunciation Guide

Bakhita: buh-KEE-tuh

Cecchini: chuh-KEE-nee

Chinon: shee-NAAN

Cristo Negro: KREE-stoh NAY-groh

Daule: DOW-lay

Ecuador: eh-kwah-DOHR

Guayabo: gwaa-JAH-boh

Guayaquil: gwaa-juh-KEEL

Hacienda: ah-see-EN-dah

Kateri Tekakwitha: GAH-deh-lee deh-gah-GWEE-tah (*Mohawk*)
kuh-TAY-ree tuh-KAW-kwih-thuh (*Anglicized*)

Lucy Yi Zhenmei: LOO-see yee juhn-MAY

Mission du Sault: mi-see-AHN doo SAHL

Narcisa de Jesús: nahr-SI-suh deh hay-SOOS

Olgossa: ohl-GAH-suh

Orléans: OR-lay-ahn

Sichuan: sih-CHWAHN

Silvania: sihl-VAH-nee-uh

Thérèse of Lisieux: tay-REZ of lee-SEE-eu

Acknowledgments:

Eduardo Garza, Cecilia Garza, Shauna'h Fuegen, Nicholas Lau, Barbara Lisette, Cynthia Schmidt, Tom Catena, Francis Gene Catena, Nasima Catena, and Nicole Lataif-Abi Kheirs

FABIOLA

About Fabiola Garza

Fabiola is an artist and author living in Orlando, FL. She graduated from Rhode Island School of Design in 2009, and has worked on video games, toys, and books. Currently, she works as a Character Artist at Disney Creative Group. Her work includes *The Story of Saint John Paul II: A Boy Who Became Pope*, Disney/Pixar's Little Golden Book *Coco*, and the cover for *A Portrait of Walt Disney World: 50 Years of the Most Magical Place on Earth*.

Fabiola is also a Princess of Heaven in training. Though her crown is often crooked, she hopes God's grace will help her soul shine. She has a great affinity for unicorns, France, and dresses with puffed sleeves.

For more of her work, please follow on Instagram
fabiolagarzacreates